FLORIOGRAPHIC

✤ SECRET ✤
GARDEN

FLORIOGRAPHIC
⋄ SECRET ⋄
GARDEN

An Artist's Coloring Book of the Hidden Language of Flowers

Vasilisa Romanenko

CASTLE POINT BOOKS
NEW YORK

Memories of childhood
were the dreams that stayed
with you after you woke.

—JULIAN BARNES

There is a place inside commingled dreams and memories where swings
still invite soaring to the stars. **Magnolia** trees welcome climbing into their
majestic embrace to find purity, strength, and stability in recollection but also
perseverance and good fortune branching out into the future. **Lilies** tickle bare
legs as the flowers take over even meticulously planned paths with their childlike
energy and optimism. **Forget-me-nots** bring back pinkie promises and the power
of staying true and faithful to love. Nature invites some treading into the past to
gather an everlasting bouquet of sweetness and goodness to bring into the now.

All things entail rising and falling timing.
You must be able to discern this.

—MIYAMOTO MUSASHI

Within the glass, time is protected. Fall-blooming **asters**, with their daisylike petals,
whisper their wisdom to be patient and have faith. Bright stars will appear in surprising
places—just as in the legend that aster flowers were born of the Greek goddess
Astraea's tears when she saw that there were no stars on earth. **Cosmos**, with their
exquisitely arranged petals, call out to believe in order and harmony. Flowers trust
in the universe's timing. Each flower of a connected plant blooms in its own time,
in its own direction, in its own space. The resulting beauty is beyond prediction.

Love does not consist in gazing
at each other, but in looking outward
together in the same direction.

—Antoine de Saint-Exupéry

In this secret spot, love is laid bare. **Bleeding hearts** confess feelings that have been hidden until this moment. Their vulnerable, heart-shaped petals dare to reach out from a strong stem and hope for a return of affection. Full, balanced layers of **camellia** petals, in colors from admiring pink to fiery red, embrace the evolution of feelings and promise faithfulness and everlasting love. A classic and enduring floral symbol, the **rose** celebrates new beginnings in white and revels in devoted, passionate love in crimson.

Life is like riding a bicycle.
To keep your balance,
you must keep moving.

—ALBERT EINSTEIN

Just when the wheels feel forever stuck in the mud, release comes. Although the way out may not be perfectly clean, narrow ribbons of light gradually widen and reveal a path ahead. **Grape hyacinths**, with their vibrant blue and purple flowers spiking upward, showcase a new season of growth. Whatever harsh conditions or wrong turns made a tangle of everything, all that is now in the past. Movement is forward and filled with promise. With basketed **anemone** blossoms leading the way, bad energy is brushed aside like a meddling hanging branch. Wide-open petals mirror a wide-open mind and heart. Tomorrow awaits.

You were wild once.
Don't let them tame you.

—ISADORA DUNCAN

It's never too late to embrace possibility. **Angelica** clusters, reaching as high as seven feet, forever seek divine inspiration and imaginative answers. The flowers were a legendary cure for the plague that an angel delivered in a dream. **Poppies**, especially in purple hues, also guide discovery through dreams. Daring to stick out their necks of blue flowers, **delphiniums** show how beautiful stretching into new experiences can be. Enduring **columbines** won't be tamed, thriving at risky heights in alpine settings with their starlike petals. Fiery **dahlias** burst with energy to spark creative journeys. Cone-shaped **larch** flowers with their many layers instill protection and confidence to grow into wild but wonderful spaces.

There are no ordinary people.
You have never talked
to a mere mortal.

—C. S. Lewis

People and flowers are never ordinary. Every bloom, no matter its size or simplicity, is beautiful and seen. With its asymmetrical flowers, the modest **violet** graces any setting with understated elegance. Its heart-shaped leaves promise faithfulness so deep that it is almost sacred. The unassuming **buttercup** bathes its surroundings—often, entire fields—in a golden glow, inspiring childlike wonder and awe. Meanwhile, the dainty **bluebell** bows gracefully as if in acknowledgment of the vast beauty that surrounds it in nature. Its humility and notoriously slow growth, especially for a wildflower, make it ever more endearing. Each flower offers gifts to cherish.

Decision is a risk
rooted in the courage
of being free.

—PAUL TILLICH

Navigating decisions often intertwines with the dance of avoidance, yet within
the realm of choices blooms a beautiful freedom. Embracing even the most
challenging decisions leads to open fields of possibility. With clusters of wisdom
and thoughtfulness, the **salvia** flower rises up with gentle guidance in decision-
making. It points upward, encouraging movement and growth. Also connected
to healing, the salvia encourages self-forgiveness for decisions that do not turn
out as expected. **Jacaranda**, with its bold blossoms, holds not just wisdom but
also the courage to make decisions. Together, they reveal the beauty inherent
in making brave choices and the grace available in starting anew as needed.

In the sweetness of friendship,
let there be laughter,
and sharing of pleasures.
For in the dew of little things
the heart finds its morning
and is refreshed.

—KHALIL GIBRAN

Hearts can be awakened in simple ways. The lilt of a songbird fills the air
with celebration on an otherwise ordinary day. A hand-signed card shares
affectionate care. **Gardenias**, with their ivory petals and intoxicating fragrance,
are a reminder to pause, breathe deeply, and appreciate beauty. Their delicate
appearance conceals a robust resilience, much like the enduring joy found in life's
small moments. Although traditionally given as a confession of love, gardenias
simply say, "You are lovely"—a sentiment worth carrying into each new day.

Truth isn't always beauty, but the hunger for it is.

—NADINE GORDIMER

In the heart's yearning, a sacred desire unfolds—a longing for what truly matters to emerge pristine from murky waters, like the legendary **lotus**. Yet the flower reveals that seeking clarity is an odyssey. Often called the "Beautiful Survivor," the lotus thrusts through muddy darkness to rise toward the sun's guiding light. Upon breaching the surface, petals unfurl one by one, stretching for enlightenment and rebirth. A purity of spirit ultimately emerges as remnants of the past wash away. As the lotus flourishes, so does love and life rooted in the genuine and transformative power of persistence toward light. Amidst life's uncertainties, the lotus offers a hopeful path to transcendence.

Hearts may break, but hearts
are the toughest of muscles,
able to pump for a lifetime,
seventy times a minute,
and scarcely falter along the way.

—Neil Gaiman

Sometimes beautiful blooming possibility hits a wall. Seeds of love are planted, but the conditions just aren't right. The hardest and healthiest step is to feel the ground underfoot, let past love's petals lightly touch the skin one last time, and then walk away. As the **bleeding heart** flowers fade from sight with time and distance, so does the lamenting heart. A new garden awaits. Just like **daffodils**, love will emerge again, vibrant and golden, in the right season and natural place. And that bloom may be ever stronger for coming through the dirt and rocks of heartache.

The beginning is always today.

—MARY WOLLSTONECRAFT SHELLEY

Fresh starts and healthy boundaries are within sight. **Mallow** flowers, with their soft, velvety petals, point to the tender dawn rising. Since ancient times, their edible gifts have offered sustenance for survival in even the harshest famine conditions. Today, mallows are often planted near homes, creating a comforting aura while maintaining their own vitality. These annuals thrive year after year by self-seeding. A self-love story in hues of pink and lavender, mallows are a reminder of the delicate dance between protection and growth. Similarly, **yarrow's** delicate clusters and feathery leaves shelter hearts from harm. This aromatic herb is strong as a guardian against mistreatment yet soft enough to welcome benevolent approach.

A playful path is the
shortest road to happiness.

—BERNIE DE KOVEN

"Climbing the ladder" doesn't need to conjure images of stiff business
attire and late nights at the office. A whimsical ring of **daisies** extends an
invitation to climb above time and traffic, swing open the door to play, and
rediscover the joy of childlike wonder. Light-hearted **larkspurs** reach for the
sky like a child stretching on tiptoes trying to touch cotton candy clouds.
Seeing the world from high in the treetops can bring fresh perspective
and energy even after feet find their way back to solid ground again.

The secret to walkin' on water
is knowing where the rocks are.

—BOOTSY COLLINS

Rocks, steadfast through boggy patches and rushing waters, often go unnoticed along everyday paths. Yet **sweet william** showers the steady tower of rocks with admiration and gratitude. The vibrant clusters of up to thirty flowers, each with five ruffled petals, express appreciation of solid support and unwavering strength. The unspoken language of sweet william honors the gallantry of those often overlooked rocks that guide through life's diverse landscapes and make each step a little easier and sweeter.

You didn't come into this world.
You came out of it,
like a wave from the ocean.
You are not a stranger here.

—ALAN WATTS

Nature is always waiting to be a guide to home. With a verdant embrace of foliage, **anthurium** flowers extend a warm welcome. The vibrant blooms dance with joy and invite shared moments. Meanwhile, the serene **peace lily** whispers messages of tranquility, purity, and healing. Its graceful presence, akin to a gentle touch, transforms spaces into sanctuaries. Together they invite sitting serenely in a place of comfort and happiness, where sunlight touches the soul and all feels right in the world.

I find the great thing in the world
is not so much where we stand,
as in what direction we are moving.

—Oliver Wendell Holmes

A strong start sets the path for an enduring journey. But the first step need
not be physical; defining the direction is a tender initiation. The bright
flowers of the **bee balm** call out to be a companion on any adventure. Named
for its ability to soothe, this floral ally promises not only broad protection
but also the bountiful gifts of health, wealth, and prosperity. The firework-
like blossoms spark energy and strength, and guide decisions by boosting
clarity of thought. No wonder bee balm was cherished as an essential plant
in the sweat lodge ceremonies of East Coast Native American tribes.

Jump, and you will find out
how to unfold your wings as you fall.

—RAY BRADBURY

In a leap of faith, two people fall in love. No one knows for sure what
will come next. Passionate red **roses** at the center of the rendezvous
profess that love is strong enough to overcome any obstacles. As hearts
open to possibility, sturdy branches of **eucalyptus** tucked into the
bouquet offer protection. Clusters of **chamomile** ground and surround
new vulnerability with calm and positive energy. The flowers bring a
wish for friendship and unity to balance the rush of romance.

A home is a kingdom of its own
in the midst of the world, a stronghold amid
life's storms and stresses,
a refuge, even a sanctuary.

—Dietrich Bonhoeffer

It's lovely to feel a rush of peace at the sight of a familiar door. Amidst the allure of exotic destinations, there is pure magic in returning to a quiet haven. The soft, silver-green leaves of **olive** branches embrace that tranquil essence and extend welcome to those who approach seeking rest and connection. Rooted in ancient Greco-Roman tales, the branches carry a tradition of peace and friendship. The delicate, pristine umbels of **Queen Anne's lace**, sometimes called bird's nest, offer warmth and sanctuary from the world's weariness. The flower has been found blooming even in abandoned lots and fields once scarred by flames.

There is always light,
if only we're brave enough to see it.
If only we're brave enough to be it.

—Amanda Gorman

In an everchanging world, **freesia** celebrates unwavering friendship—the kind that illuminates what truly matters and serves as a steadying light. The flower's name is even a salute to relationships: botanist Christian F. Ecklon named the flower after his friend and fellow botanist Friedrich H. T. Freese. Each fragrant blossom promises to stay near at heart and offers to help lift daily stresses. One of the most popular flowers in the world, freesias (like friendship) are challenging to grow and their petals are extremely delicate, requiring careful handling. Just as freesia blossoms open with grace, true friends unfold in our lives. Their vibrant presence becomes a constant reminder of support and a reliable source of joy.

The most important thing in life
is to learn how to give out love,
and to let it come in.

—MORRIE SCHWARTZ

Love will come where there is hope. An open gate bordered on the outside by
uplifted celestial blue **cornflowers** signals an open heart. Often called bachelor's
buttons, these flowers, once placed in the buttonholes of Victorian suitors,
now adorn the entry as tokens of anticipation. Flagstones invite a slow, step-
by-step entry into relationship and intimacy. Clusters of **lilac** flowers, reaching
eagerly beyond the gate, mirror the essence of new or first love, a delicate yet
passionate stretch toward the unknown. The balance between boundaries
and welcoming path sets a beautiful scene of giving and accepting love.

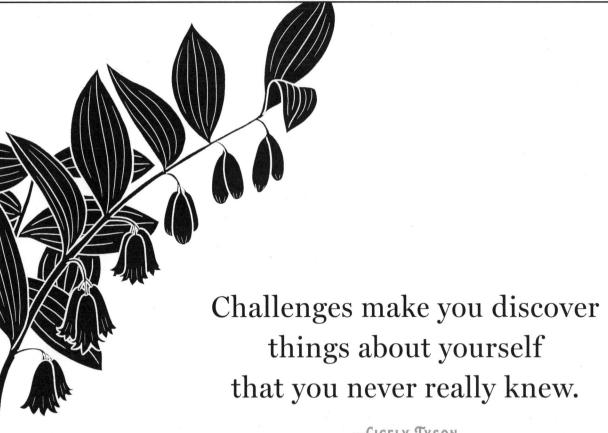

Challenges make you discover
things about yourself
that you never really knew.

—CICELY TYSON

The stops in life can start a process of seeking. Barriers can transform
into gateways to profound revelations when met with an openness to new
paths. Looking back, the once certain route may reveal itself as lacking in
the refreshment sought. **Iris** blooms thrive near a source of fresh water,
wisely pointing to the need for flowing inspiration. **Solomon's seals**, delicate
tubes on arching stems, reach into their surroundings, adapting effortlessly.
The round imprints on their roots, reminiscent of King Solomon's ancient
seal, celebrate inner wisdom, deepening with each life experience.

Many of us have made
our world so familiar that
we do not see it anymore.

—John O'Donohue

There is magic to be discovered through wandering off the busy, beaten path.
Beneath their tranquil canopy, cascading **wisteria** blossoms offer refuge
for quiet reflection. The flower's slow, deliberate growth while establishing
roots in its early years brings to life the truth that beautiful transformation
is often gradual, after a time of grounding. Patience will pay off in blooms
that showcase deep strength and offer enlightenment for others who travel
along a similar path. Underneath wisteria's enchanting embrace is a place
to slow the pace, ponder life's mysteries, and recognize innermost truths.

Some of us think
holding on makes us strong,
but sometimes it is letting go.

—Hermann Hesse

The time has come to close a door. Cascading **morning glories** make their
presence and affection known but remain gentle in their touch, allowing
for separation and saying goodbye. While some vines seem invasive
and strangling in their hold, these beauties are sweet in their clinging as
in an embrace. Spiky **hyssop** salutes new beginnings as past pages are
cleanly turned. With nothing expected in return, **gardenias** send pure
wishes for joy on the journey. The delicate blooms and fresh scent ward
off negative energy. Steps away and forward will be with no regrets.

Keep your face always
toward the sunshine—
and shadows will
fall behind you.

—WALT WHITMAN

Sunflowers are wise. Rarely do they grow in isolation; they thrive in community.
Yet no matter how densely packed into a field, each bloom seeks a greater warmth
and sustaining light as it lifts its head to the sun above. They stretch for what
they need without encroaching on a neighboring flower's space. Sharing joy
through their full, vibrant yellow-and-orange blooms, sunflowers spread seeds of
positivity and strength far and wide. But it's not a head-in-the-clouds optimism
that is easily crumpled; the flowers grow high supported by sturdy stems.

New beginnings
are often disguised
as painful endings.

—Lao Tzu

Hidden beneath the surface lies a reservoir of beauty and vitality. Like brilliant fish concealed in a muddied pond until the perfect sunlight angle unveils their splendor, mysteries often await discovery. **Calla lilies** too hold a deep surprise: the elegant trumpet that they are popularly recognized by is not their flower. Although still beautiful, the tube is actually a spathe, a modified leaf used to protect a flower's reproductive system. The true flower is a cluster nestled within the plant. Nature reveals that exquisite promises and second chances may be concealed within, waiting to be grasped at just the right time.

A little flower that blooms in May.
A lovely sunset at the end of a day.
Someone helping a stranger along the way.
That's heaven to me.

—Sam Cooke

The treasure that's worth the most should be simple to find without a map. It's all around and within. True gold is living and blooming, as brilliant as the daisylike flowers of the **gazania** in summer oranges and yellows. True gold is in the heart, opening to the sun with the energy of a **California poppy** and spreading like the wildflower it is. True gold fills in the empty places with positivity, like the star-shaped petals of sprawling **pentas** that bloom even in the deep of winter in some places. Flowers point to riches that can't be contained.

The decisions you make
are a choice of values
that reflect your life in every way.

—ALICE WATERS

Every moment is a choice. The sheltering boughs of a blossoming **apple** tree offer space to ponder the passage of time and the path that has led to this particular place. As the fleeting blossoms showcase the beauty of cycles, they gently urge us to savor the beauty of now, to commit to the shared joy of the present. That's not to say that the next stage won't be filled with hope and fruitfulness of its own. But in this breath, nature asks that we make the choice to spend time together and appreciate the splendor within sight, rather than jumping ahead to seasons that can't be predicted. Thoughts are meant to stay close and connected, like the velvety petals of deep-hued **pansies** that murmur, "Thinking of you."

Love recognizes no barriers.
It jumps hurdles, leaps fences,
penetrates walls to arrive
at its destination full of hope.

—MAYA ANGELOU

As refreshing as it can be to jump into a cool stream, hearts need steady ground in which to root and grow. The flowering **dogwood** stands as a testament to enduring love, strong against suddenly developing winds and swiftly moving waters. Its delicate blossoms whisper words of unwavering commitment and promise rest from the rocky currents. Just as the dogwood blooms perennially with tending, love can remain in bloom through the many seasons of life. A steadfast bond, as supportive and safe as a well-constructed bridge, can prevail over all kinds of terrain and tribulations along the wondrous journey.

Our greatest glory is
not in never falling,
but in rising
every time we fall.

—Confucius

Life reveals hidden depths beyond first impressions. Seemingly desolate places can burst into bloom, and people who appear defeated often unveil resilience. Experiences, initially perceived as empty or even devastating, can resonate with profound meaning. Among the oldest flowering plants on earth, **protea** share their wisdom to explore life's intricate layers. Named after Proteus, the shape-shifting Greek god, the protea survives in extreme conditions and regenerates itself after wildfires, pointing to a hope that lasts beyond any current situation and the possibility for transformation. Its blossoms gracefully re-emerge, embodying the courage of finding meaning in the process of recovery and rebuilding. Sweetly scented **lily of the valley** reaches beyond mere survival, promising a return to happiness. It is a fragrant reminder that joy persists, even within the trials of life.

You must love in such a way
that the person you love feels free.

—Thích Nhất Hạnh

Unselfish love wants to open the world to those close at heart. That may
mean letting go and saying goodbye for a time. A full bouquet of white
and pink **carnations** extends an empowering (not constricting) embrace
and unconditional care, like that of a parent who fully trusts that distance
will not separate hearts and minds. The addition of **heather** flowers sends
luck and protection for the journey ahead. Together, the blooms share that
home is always waiting with an open door and without emotional chains.

Forever—is composed of Nows.

—EMILY DICKINSON

Steps slow under the **cherry** blossoms. The world is painted in a peaceful cloud of delicate pinks and whites. Each cascading petal above and each stepping stone below feels infinite. Yet the blossoms' season is short—a reminder to take in joy when it comes, as long as it lasts. No photos, no posting, no comments: the beauty is meant to be embraced in this quiet moment. Any worries about the next season fall away, and this season is allowed to make an honorable exit in its time.

Sometimes I think,
I need a spare heart
to feel all the things I feel.

—SANOBER KHAN

Emotions can be difficult to contain. Perhaps that is because they are not meant to be sealed away forever. Much of the unique beauty of the sprawling **fuchsia** flower lies in how its abundant petals and stamen spill out like confiding love. Deep emotions are free to cascade in a wild but natural way, reaching for a place to touch and spark a little magic. **Forget-me-nots** balance the whimsical nature of the fuchsia, declaring that the passionate feelings are not simply for a season: a heart has been stamped forever.

We don't even know how strong
we are until we are forced to bring
that hidden strength forward.

—ISABEL ALLENDE

It's simple to make a wish and put confidence in the toss of a coin. The risk
is low and the effort is comfortable. But the greater reward comes from
reaching down deep and pulling up from a well of strength, even on days
when the bucket seems empty. In fact, the bucket may bring to the surface
a surprising bouquet of renewal, spirit, and confidence as intoxicating as
the scent of **lilacs**. With inner tending, the possibilities for healing and
prosperity are as large and lush as **peonies**, just waiting to be gathered.

Happiness is not a matter of
intensity but of balance, order,
rhythm and harmony.

—THOMAS MERTON

Beauty lies in balance. The exotic **orchid** stands tall in confidence, its elegant petals reaching for the pinnacle of luxury and grace. Yet it is only an enduring flower when given consistent tender care. Its requirements are a reminder that any lasting bloom depends on nurturing. **Ferns** are quite different—happy to unceremoniously unfurl their fronds. In fact, the plant's humility is sometimes linked with legends of invisibility. Magic exists in both grand gestures and quiet growth alike. It flows forth with care of, and connection to, the sincere self.

The strongest love is the love
that can demonstrate its fragility.

—Paulo Coelho

Love can be strong, and love can be fragile. Love is at its best when it is both at the same time. Tender **cyclamens** carpet woodlands with an enchanting effect, yet they are tougher than they appear. The flowers and their foliage remain strong and bounce back even where feet and celebratory picnics tread. Thanks to its tuber, which allows it to withstand difficult conditions, the captivating cyclamen shows resilience and celebrates the power of deep, lasting love.

A garden is a friend
you can visit any time.

—Okakura Kakuzo

A friendship is also a garden you can visit anytime. Like the intricate layers of a **zinnia** flower, friendship unfolds, each distinctly hued petal of a memory revealing shared laughter and cherished moments. As the blooms spread yet remain intertwined, the connection deepens, creating a timeless tapestry of affection that withstands the seasons of life and any physical separation. **Tiger lilies**, bold and untamed, mirror the fierce loyalty of friendship. Just as their petals stand tall, a strong bond rises above challenges. In the aromatic embrace of **eucalyptus**, friendship thrives. Sturdy branches shield delicate leaves and celebrate the enduring essence of bound hearts.

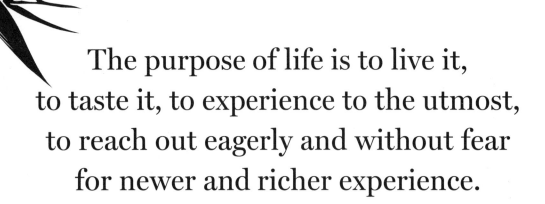

The purpose of life is to live it,
to taste it, to experience to the utmost,
to reach out eagerly and without fear
for newer and richer experience.

—ELEANOR ROOSEVELT

Passion can burst forth in surprising directions. The feeling can be unfamiliar at first, and tempting to push back, but beautiful growth is not meant to be contained. The vivid blooms and exuberant foliage of the **bird of paradise** know no bounds. The exotic plant's uplifted flowers appear ready to take flight into worlds of adventure where every heartbeat is a cue to dance and every moment is an invitation to untamed joy. All that's needed is an open door.

True love is eternal, infinite, and
always like itself. It is equal and pure,
without violent demonstrations:
it is seen with white hairs and
is always young in the heart.

—Honoré de Balzac

Passion meets promise. Romance advances to relationship. Spontaneous
words become eternal vows. Lasting love is sealed among the **tulips**
that celebrate the declared commitment with their tenderly unfolding
blooms. The delicate **periwinkle** above keeps faithfulness and trust in
focus, a reminder that enduring love thrives on unwavering loyalty.
Ivy tendrils cling to the sturdy support, bringing wishes of fidelity and
attachment. Nature rejoices at the evolution of love—the development
of an intimate bond that feels both ages old and new every day.

We get no choice.
If we love, we grieve.

—Thomas Lynch

Although grief is an inevitable part of the journey of a connected life, no orderly path walks through the emotions. Moving through a loss can feel like heavy pots of overflowing mourning some days. Other days, with a closer look, the vibrant **marigolds** within the pots reflect the warmth and energy of tender memories. Fragrant **rosemary** can prompt remembrances that uplift with sweetness or pull too far into the past and regret. In the meandering passage through grief can come an honoring of the mix of emotions. With careful tending to the soul's garden, spiritual calm will one day break through like delicate yet unyielding **alyssum** that rises through cracks in the pavement.

To confront a person
with his shadow
is to show him his own light.

—CARL JUNG

Courage resides in unveiling truths and illuminating past wrongs. Embarking on a
new path demands revisiting the juncture where trust faltered. **Lavender**, with its
calming essence, invites a dialogue to put feelings of betrayal on the table. The flower's
connection to distrust came through the Victorians, who believed Cleopatra was killed
by a poisonous snake that had been lurking under a lavender bush. The Egyptian queen
was also known to use lavender as a tool of seduction. At the same time, the flower's
healing properties introduce the possibility of reconciliation in a scarred relationship.
Fingerlike blooms of **foxglove** point the conversation toward resolving secrets. Just as
these fragile blooms benefit from support, a friendship flourishes when stabilized.

There was never a night or a problem
that could defeat sunrise or hope.

—BERNARD WILLIAMS

When nights seem long, unending even, nature holds hope. Sunrise is ever
on the horizon. Flowers continue to bloom in the dark. Hardy **hellebores**
thrive in shaded woodlands and grace the coldest months with enchanting
blossoms. The magical, saucer-shaped flowers, related to buttercups, defy
unfavorable conditions and attract pollinators with their early-season dreams.
Clover, nestled beneath wandering feet, sprinkle the path with hope,
casting wishes of luck in every direction the day's journey takes.

Take forgiveness slowly.
Don't blame yourself for being slow.
Peace will come.

—Yoko Ono

Although the flight toward forgiveness seems steep, the first step itself is often the most dreaded hurdle. Sweetly scented **hyacinths** pave the way toward healing. The uplifted blooms extend a balm of courage to seek or extend forgiveness with sincere intent. On the path of reconciliation, regrets fade away like handpicked **rue** flowers strewn aside at the end of a child's playday. Each move forward in the tender journey becomes a poignant gesture of letting go of the past and growing into understanding and renewal.

Life must be aromatic.
There must be scent, somehow
there must be some.

—GWENDOLYN BROOKS

Scent awakens the soul. The sweet fragrance of **jasmine** is an intoxicating
nudge to buy the flowers and the champagne, to throw arms around
the world. Night-blooming jasmine's zest for life and quest for sensual
experience cannot be contained; it spreads like a wildflower in its passion.
Yet within its unassuming beauty lies an invitation to savor the simple
and seemingly ordinary. The star-shaped petals of jasmine, a perpetual
celebration, pull hearts and minds into the romantic dance of life.
Each moment becomes a toast to enchantment found in the everyday.

You can't see the future coming—not the terrors, for sure, but you also can't see the wonders that are coming, the moments of light-soaked joy that await each of us.

—JOHN GREEN

It's natural to hold at least a little fear of the unknown. But there can also be space for excitement at what could be around the next corner. The abundant blooms of **hydrangea** are a reminder of the fullness of life—experiences we have been through and those yet to come. The flower's ability to change from one glorious color to another equally beautiful hue based on soil pH is encouragement to adapt to changing circumstances with grace.

Life is either a daring
adventure or nothing at all.

—HELEN KELLER

When beginning a high climb, the lowest levels may be filled with abundant flowers
and lush greenery. Feet are surrounded by promise with each early step. As the journey
ascends, the prospect of stumbling may eclipse the beauty below. But the noble **edelweiss**,
growing on some of the most inaccessible mountain peaks, invites keeping up courage
and seeking unexpected blooms in challenging places. Its star-shaped flowers call out
to never lose a sense of wonder in the journey to the heights or upon arrival. While
bay laurel tends to be associated with ancient Greek wreaths and crowns of sports
victory, the common **mountain laurel**, wild in nature, reminds us of the importance of
everyday victories and daring to dream of success in whatever terms the soul desires.

Goodbyes are only for those
who love with their eyes.
Because for those who love
with heart and soul there is
no such thing as separation.

—RUMI

Goodbyes are not easy. No one wants to leave a place where beautiful blossoms surround and flowing water refreshes. But the garden of the heart can hold eternal space for all the good shared. **Sweet pea** clusters can murmur *goodbye* and *thank you* in the same floral exhalation. **Morning glories** can stay rooted in affectionate memories while climbing toward new heights. The garden of the heart is grateful for past moments that are enduring treasures and inspirations. Even seasons that seem too short leave boundless gifts.

Keep planting, sowing, living,
and knowing that beautiful things
take time. And that's okay.

—Morgan Harper Nichols

In the garden and in life, waiting for visible growth isn't easy.
The bulbs of the **amaryllis** are planted in the fall so that the stunning
trumpet-shaped blooms burst forth on tall stems in the winter season.
With care, amaryllis bulbs can live for up to seventy-five years, giving
flowers year after year over an entire lifetime. The longer the plant lives,
the larger the bulb grows, producing more stems with more flowers.
The initial wait and ongoing nurture is worth decades of beautiful gifts.